Composite Sketches

Composite Sketches

by

Lou Orfanella

Fine Tooth Press

For Justin Matthew and Marygrace Faith

May I one day deserve you.

Love,

Dad

Acknowledgements

I like to think of my poems as composite sketches, mosaics made up of fragments of what was and what might have been. People and places, time and space, fact and fantasy, all converge at some distant vanishing point to create an image of what we like to think of as self. I am eternally grateful to those who contributed to, and were a part of, the events that led to the creation of these poems and the poet, especially Marie, who made the journey better than I ever imagined. Thanks also to my students at Western Connecticut State University in the Fall of 2003 who helped workshop some of these poems, to Oscar De Los Santos for his enthusiastic support, and to Ivana Masic, whose talent made the cover art all I had envisioned and more.

A good number of the poems in this collection originally appeared in the following limited edition chapbooks: *The Last Automat* (Argonne House Press, 2001), *Summer Rising, River Flowing* (Pudding House Publications, 2003), and *Permanent Records* (Argonne House Press, 2003). Additionally, "The Last Automat" appeared in *The Danbury News-Times*, "Charcoal Drawings in the Park" in *English Journal* and *WordWrights!*, "Composite Sketch" in *WordWrights!*, and "Rising," "Leaving Anatevka," and "Disinterred" on the website http://www.agnesinnepa.org. Earlier versions of "When They Caught the Son of Sam" and "October Song" first appeared in *Poet: An International Monthly*.

Contents

Part 1: Composite Sketches

Part 2: Summer Rising, River Flowing

Part 3: K-tel Presents Believe in Poetry

Part I:

Composite Sketches

The Gatherers

The grass seemed to be made of denim as the bodies huddled together
Her clothes once made her feel unique now they made her blend in
When she called home last night a peaceful protest is how she described it
To her mom saying nothing to her about the boy with the muscular arms
And nothing at all to her father who sends checks for tuition and food monthly

I had only seen her once or twice on campus she
Always walking with the boy with the muscular arms
Entranced by his commitment to the to the antiwar movement
Believing he would keep her safer at home than
He could in Southeast Asia where his muscular arms
Would make him the same as every soldier around him
Like her clothes made her part of the landscape of humanity

Her brown hair on his arm his blond hair touching her head
Her smile threatening to obscure the view of the angry person
With the red bandana and the tense look
It was a jarring mosaic of anger and contentment of
Joy and sorrow of truths and half-truths
The young person with the bandana appears older than the others
But is their contemporary in all ways but one having
Lived that which they have only read about

She does not know that her smile will soon fade
Believing with all her heart the poster left tacked on her
Bedroom wall in the house with the trimmed hedges and
Wooden gate the one about war not being healthy
Abbey Road was still a lifetime away the year
Sgt. Pepper played endlessly as we studied the
Collage of images on the album jacket
None looking like the angry face the face that would
Retain its intensity the anger morphing to commitment
The commitment to pride while the two others would
Take complacency to indifference then on to
Ambivalence and finally to acceptance
Looking back as if they were never there
Back to when we believed we were doing something
That mattered and that would change the world

Action News

"Action News was also about the heart of a city, of a people, of each of us."
-Jeff Kamen, former anchor/reporter WPIX Action News

Back then you turned on the ten o'clock news on channel eleven
Not sure if you were an hour ahead of the eleven o'clock reports
Or four hours behind the six o'clock broadcasts on the other channels
You waited as the theme music built to a crescendo before its cold end
You craved more than what you saw in the twenty second sound bites
That teased during the *Eight O'Clock Movie* back in the days when
Reporters stepped from vans with faded station logos on the side
Camera, light, and sound technicians off screen as the
Ubiquitous reporter asked the unanswerable questions

It was about covering the stories that really mattered
The bacteria encrusted hospital wards where the sick got sicker
The mental health facilities where minds and spirits were broken
Under ream after ream of indecipherable bureaucratic files and charts
That nobody would ever read it was about
Neighborhoods where blood spilled in the streets and children
Played and died in alleys and about the social injustices that
Defined who we were and who we might become

It was not about the tattooed half-naked bleached blond
Lip-syncing thong wearing prefabricated stars with
Their bevy of bare behinds reported on by the
Interchangeable blow dried mannequins who
Match the motif of the plastic anchor desk

The heart of a newscast lies in the people you do not know
The headlines that get buried amid the glitz glimmer and glamour
The heart of the news like the heart of the city
Is found when the music fades and the studio lights come up
The real drama of real human life when the film was
Processed and relay raced to the control room
Not the video taped reality TV voyeurism passing for news
Not the quasi-celebrities sucked dry for their fifteen minutes
By the media whores who eat them and spit them out

We know now what you knew then
Even when the consultants made you change
Your hair and the rest and you moved from
Field to anchor desk and back again
That *Action News* was so much more
It was in the final analysis the heart of us all

13

When They Caught the Son of Sam

When they caught the Son of Sam
.44 caliber serial killer stalking victims
In parked cars by night since April
Captured in the heat of a New York City August
We were in the middle of a week
Surrounded by purples and greens and blues
Canoeing in the Adirondacks along the
Chain of lakes connected by the Raquett River
Big Tupper, Little Tupper, Simon's Pond, Long Lake

We set out on Sunday from the dock at
Raquett Lake with our five metal canoes
And one oversized red kayak
During my first season of seventeen
We had no thoughts of the Son of Sam
As he lurked in dark alleys so many miles to our south
While we canoed north
That seemed odd but we did canoe north
An entourage of thirteen we put on
Bright orange life jackets and a variety of caps
My denim camping hat which I used for nothing else
Darryl's Huck Finn hat, Mark's Picasso hat
Mr. Lambert put on a leather hat with a wide brim
Then sealed his toilet paper and cigarettes in a Ziplock
Preacher wore a red bandana
Rob put on a pair of sunglasses that you could
See out of but not into, the kind with mirrors

By late afternoon we would set up camp
Along the riverbank or beside one of the lakes
Canoes pulled ashore orange and blue tents
Pitched clotheslines strung to air out
Sleeping bags and wet clothes
Every new stop quickly becoming home
There was nothing particularly romantic about
What we were doing no Walden's Pond
Back to nature philosophy although the beaver dam
That seemed a mile long added a sense of awe
We were in reality just a bunch of
Guys in the rustic outskirts of northern New York
Who would too soon return to school or jobs

As the sun would sink lower in the sky
Shadows etching the smooth surface
We would turn the clear lake water into a
Turkish bathhouse wading in with our
Little plastic tubes of biodegradable soap
Worked to a weak lather on our hair and skin
Soap then floating upstream or was it downstream
I know we canoed north which seemed odd

Later when we had eaten a dinner cooked
On propane stoves next to campfires in rings of stones
And had drunk iced tea made from powder mixed
With lake water in a five gallon plastic jug
Mr. Lambert and I, not yet ready to rest
Would slide a canoe back into the water
And paddle around at twilight comfortable
Black fly season over and heat of the day behind us

When the sun rose each morning we would again
Load the canoes Rob in the bow, I in the stern
Ready for the miles of paddling and portages
Around sections too rocky for our canoes
Journeys temporarily replacing cruising to the Windmill Diner
For cheeseburgers and onion rings and Cokes
Most days the weather was good although we did get
Caught in a storm in the oxbow where we huddled in
Vinyl ponchos under a grove of trees
After carefully traversing Simon's Pond
Taking on water and trying not to get hit broadside

I grew my first beard that week since removing
The original stubble at thirteen
We had not seen a newspaper or heard a radio
No forecasts or hints about how the Yankees were doing
Although Darryl and I discussed it frequently while
Rob pined for his Mets
On Thursday, our fifth day out
We canoed from the lean-to where we spent our
Last couple of nights to a village across the lake where
None of the shops had familiar names
There was a Salvation Army store that sold things
Like Huck Finn hats
It was there all those miles from New York City
That someone told us
They caught The Son of Sam

15

Tales of the Sour Cream Sierras

1. Signs

I always wondered on the drive up Route 17
How anybody who did not have the same destination
Every year or had never been there at all
Made a decision about where to go
The billboards telling you the number of miles to
Resorts, hotels, lodges, and bungalow colonies
All looked the same and the signs made up of smaller signs
Looked like rows of the license plates we would read
On the way up from the city looking for obscure states
But always finding the same few words on the signs
Meaning no more than the jumble of letters and numbers
On the plates then still more signs lined up along the
Road like advertisements on outfield walls
The only sign that mattered was the one that read
"Red Apple Rest" in Southfield where we would stop
During the crowded ride to the bungalow if we
Needed to "go" sooner we knew to hold it and keep
Quiet about it no unscheduled stops allowed
Me and my brother and two cousins lining up at
The long rows of adjacent urinals to see who could
Pee from the farthest or for the longest
Someone's KEDS always getting wet
It never made sense to stop so close to the end of the trip
Maybe one meal prepared by someone else before
Unpacking the boxes of food and utensils

2. Trains

Every year taking the train north from the city
We would pass a rundown barn that always seemed
To lean a bit to one side
Every summer the wood seemed more weathered
The lilt a bit more pronounced
It was a strange attraction to look forward to but
We always did there were never any
Animals around the tilting old barn and only
Once did we see a person nearby
He did not seem to belong there but more
Like he was just passing through as transitory
As we were when the year finally came
That the old barn was on its side so too came
The end of the innocence that had always been
Part of the summer we were older now
Too old for the carefree days of July and August
We were bigger in body and in how we saw
The world cozy became cramped
I can still see those valises and shopping bags
Crowding us in the seats we barely moving
Except for a turn at the window seat
Adventure turned to monotony
Street corners called more than the
Crickets and whippoorwills
It was the last time we took that train
The last time we saw that barn
The beginning of a life that was as
Foreign as a farmyard on a city street

3. Blisters

There was that one day each summer when
Everyone else was outside and I had to
Stay in because of the blistering sunburn
Across my shoulders, back, and tops of my feet
That I would get every year not willing to
Slowly get used to the sun or wear a
Shirt and sneakers I had to feel that
Complete freedom the very first day
The previous year's burn a faded memory
Painted from head to toe with cold cream
Trying to sleep without touching the bed
Never with the foresight to remember
I was losing more than I gained
A bright red layer of skin lifted off in big
Stringy sheets the slimy globs of Noxema that
Temporarily extinguished the burning
Sensation Dad arriving from the city on
Friday with the look and head shake that
Said, "You did it again," with no words at all

4. Rowboats

Every summer the rowboats waited for us at the
Lake never repainted they would be chained to
Long metal spikes driven into the ground
The boats differed from each other only by the
Initials scraped into them with sharp sticks
Yet we would look for the same one all the time
We would put the ores in place and take turns
Rowing across the lake in a straight line
Almost always making a big circle being
Stronger in one arm than the other
As the years went on we would take the
Boats out later and later fewer of us at
Twilight and fewer still after dark when
Mosquitoes would draw our blood and leave
Their irregularly shaped welts
Moonlight was the only path to follow to the
Other side I reached only once finding an
Image forever remaining in my memory as the
Girl across the lake with a flashlight and box of
Fig Newtons a composite of every girl I would
Ever meet or dream of meeting in the
Moonlight or in the dark

5. The Sullivan Show

Every one of us stole jokes from the others
Hoping to have the last laugh
Schmoozing with the guests in their ugly
Bathing suits by day so they could tell their
Friends they met us as if it mattered
My act was not all that bad for a tummler
And a living was a living
From the stage I would focus on the
Single face alone at the third table from
Stage left she would be looking too although
Our eyes never quite seemed to meet
Some day they would, just as some day
I would make the drive ninety miles
Southeast and never look back like
Red Buttons and Sid Caesar and Danny Kaye and
Milton Berle and Alan King and Morey
Amsterdam and of course Henny Youngman
Before me knowing it would happen every time
Another season another year as the laughter came
Drowning out the clinking ice cubes hushed
Murmurings as the booking agents for
The Ed Sullivan Show looked on readying my
Slot between Kate Smith and Senor Wences
Live on a Sunday night after *The Jack Benny
Program* and before *What's My Line?*

6. Gentiles and Jews

She asked me to bring some butter to the table
At breakfast when I looked into her eyes I
Would have brought her the entire cow
If I could have she had no idea that I
Could not serve her dairy at the Kosher table
Embarrassed when I told her she apologized
Profusely as if she had insulted me and
Thousands of years of culture simply by
Wanting butter on her bagel
I had her table again at dinner that night
Doing my usual smiling and laughing at guests'
Unfunny jokes that are often not worth the
Tips I received for placing bowls of
Soup and baskets of challah on the
White tablecloths she was the prettiest daughter
Of the loudest guest in the room constantly
Directing her gaze to her lap as the adults
Laughed louder but she kept her secret
Knowing they would not be laughing if they
Knew what the gentile daughter and the
Jewish waiter had done

7. A Key

When I found the antique key I knew there
Was a story it was rusty and tarnished
As it lay almost unnoticed in the rubble of
The dusty hallway of the abandoned hotel
It was not the type of key that would fit a
Door but more the kind that went to one of
Those wooden trunks or perhaps a hutch
Where there was a desk that closed up and
Had windowed doors above it where
China and knickknacks were kept and
Locked at the end of the day
Demolition was scheduled for the end of the
Week I would have to canvass the entire
Building and the others around it to see
What the key might open furniture removed
Over the last couple of weeks and sold at auction
My chance of finding something the key would
Open would be in the basements, storage rooms,
Caretaker cottages surrounding the main building
I could not explain the attraction of the key the
Obsession it was breeding any more than
One can explain the attraction between two
Strangers separated by life and commitment
Pulled together by a force stronger than both

8. The Last Resort

The first and the last of the great Catskill resorts
Facing extinction with empty rooms unpaid creditors
The signs were there as clearly as the signs along
Route 17 for roadside sales and little diners
Whether it was hope or denial nobody really knows
Whatever it was we ignored the signs always believing
The Concord and the rest of the Catskill royalty
Grossinger's, The Stevensville, The Nevele
Would always remain always find a way to go on
That the lavish meals in the kitchen after the guests
Had retired would be there for us
They are using bulldozers and wrecking balls
Not explosives to level the hotel in the
Mountains where the past has resided with the
Present even as the last of the linens and dishes
Disappear from the second colonial America
The Jewish Alps, The Borsht Belt, The Sour
Cream Sierras where there were once as many
Bungalows as condominiums in Florida with
Many of the same inhabitants European Jews
Immigrants after the first world war who
Turned Ellenville, Liberty, and Livingston Manor
To a new world now hundreds seek work and
We go from soup in the Concord kitchen to
The community soup kitchens where they
Serve more than we ever did

Primary Sources

She is never sure how to end her poems the truth begins to
Surface then retreats back to the darkness
Yet to find its way into the hardbound notebook
Where she scribbles her secret longings
Her first journal without a tiny lock and key
One for grown up musings fantasies of lying
Beside another body gently breathing in the night
Although her nights are spent alone
She writes her poems in the semi-darkness
Rising before dawn writing beginnings and middles
But no endings sometimes she waits until the sun goes down
Staying up late until everyone else is asleep
The dampness rising through her open window
Small nightlight illuminating the blue and black ink
Streaking the barren pages sometimes she writes in red
When it is hot and sweaty other times in pencil
Making marks visible only to her
Some nights she sips tea when she writes not minding when it
Drips on her words light brown splotches marring her
Clean smooth pages making them look like the
Parchment paper of an ancient religious scroll
Other nights she eats rich dark chocolate letting it
Melt on her tongue and slide slowly down her throat
She wears very little when she writes alone in the night
Hoping to one day connect with that which lies far
Beneath her skin knowing that the secrets will bring her
Poems to life that the endings will come when one day
She is ready to face the pain of the reality that is hers alone
Like the songs of nature she hears at the window
As the rain hits the glass and the wind
Brushes the tree branch into the house
And the tears that only she knows flow when she
Lets her hair down and faces the night

Barry Manilow Doesn't Suck and Other Sound Bites

In the Olympic Diner

Justin spreads butter on his
Pancakes like an artist he
Spreads it out of the little plastic
Containers covering every spot
As if preparing a
Canvas with a layer of white paint

Parallel Universe

The Cosby Show went off the air about
Ten years ago I saw two new episodes
Last night on Nick-at-Nite
I don't think it is just that I never saw
Them in their original runs
I am not sure how they get Theo and Rudy
Young again but I have this feeling that there
Is a parallel universe where they can
Make new episodes of old shows and
Slip them unnoticed into the rerun cycle

Never Having to Say You're Sorry

I don't care about critical acclaim
I want to write something like *Love Story*
That makes people cry when the heroine
Dies or the brief romance ends on a
Bittersweet note if the critics make
Madison County analogies so be it
If Hollywood offers a check I will
Cash it and retire young
God bless America

My Grandfather's Leather Jacket

Even all these years after his death
My grandfather's leather jacket smells
Like him his closet his car
Milton (the accountant not the 17th century writer)
Once said wearing it would feel like still having
My grandfather's arms around me

Barry Manilow Doesn't Suck

Barry Manilow doesn't suck
That is what the world is realizing after
All these years his songs were
Popular standards for the seventies like
The Carpenters and Helen Reddy and John Denver
It must be nice for him to finally be hip
What with Sinatra gone

So They Can Say They Did

Most of the players on the single A
Hudson Valley Renegades will never have
That proverbial cup of coffee in the big leagues
They will forever remember the bus rides the
First time they heard their names on the PA system
Echo through the night air and the girls who
Slept with them just so they could say they did

There Were a Few Scattered Raindrops

There were a few scattered raindrops
Falling from the mostly clear sunny sky
When the tears ran down your face
They seemed equally out of place
Marring the smooth clear warmth in
Droplets of unrequited love

One Thought Leads to Another

I am reading a collection of Kathleen Norris' poems
And as is the joy of poetry one thought leads to
Another taking me to places gone and people lost
How could she take her life I remember the
Grade school innocence the nights and days of
Buying fast food from her at the McDonalds
The going away party when she moved shortly
After we had pizza following a high school dance
Learning years later that she had taken her own
Life on the west coast how could she have been
Unaware of so much

Legacy

I don't know if my father ever went to a
Baseball game with his father so much history
Is lost within two generations the stories of our
Lives gone like the dried out newspaper clippings
Taped to pages of a scrapbook I must preserve
Tonight's memory as my son forced in a run
Walked, stole a base, was hit by two pitches
As his team won the little league division
Championship which was better than any
World Series game I have ever seen

Justin's Recital

His eyes tell you he is in the zone like an
Athlete getting ready for a playoff
He sits at the piano and raises his hands
To the keyboard hitting every note and inflection
With the precision of a surgeon slicing through
Layers of flesh to expose the inner soul
While the world around him stands still

Tevye's Dream Revisited

My maternal grandmother
Visited me in a dream last night
It was like Tevye's dream in
Fiddler on the Roof but
Not scary I woke up thinking
That she looked good for having
Been dead for over ten years

Director's Cut

In all of our brains there
Is a mechanism like a movie
Camera that makes a permanent
Record of all we see do and say
We can rewind it at will but
Must adjust the focus to view
Everything clearly again if
Something is changed call it
The director's cut who but us will know

Forever New

A new practice is being floated that
Could evolve to theory eventually with
Application of scientific method wherein
Prolonged celibacy restores virginity
She feels less guilty wearing white
He feels he is getting the chaste prize
The Holy Grail the golden palace
While it is really the same old songs
Packaged to look new in the
K-tel compilation

Dog with Goggles

The golden retriever looked from side to side
Staring through his goggles that made him look
Like a barnstorming pilot or a member of
Pappy Boyington's Black Sheep Squadron
He was strapped in the sidecar of a
Motorcycle waiting for his master to emerge
From the pool supply store he did not say
Anything but looked content enough
Fleasy Rider with the wind rustling his hair

Superman Revisited

Damned if it didn't happen all over again
I never expect it but a glance and back to
Square one maybe one day I can be a
Superhero true identity known only to you
And when I change to preserve justice you can
Be there too in real life our identities would be
Reporter or poet I'll wear my glasses more often
And you can be what you are you do that
So well maybe you could be the
Superhero and I will be your loyal sidekick

Weeks Per Jew

A ninety-year-old Nazi was sentenced to
Serve another ten years for killing 667
Jews in concentration camps even if he
Lives to be 100 and started serving right
After the war which is unlikely that would
Still average to only a very unacceptable
Number of weeks per Jew

Summer Into Fall

We get just so many days years if you prefer
Like the episodes of a TV show we get renewed
For thirteen week cycles with no guarantee of
Production of all episodes at times my life
Seems like the final episode of *St. Elsewhere*
When everything took place in the imagination
Of the autistic boy in *MASH* everyone got to
Go home at the end while the ironic happened to
The WJM staff Ted staying the rest getting fired
Maybe the end will be like Bob Newhart where
His life as the Vermont innkeeper was actually a
Dream of the stammering Chicago shrink
Summer days dwindle to fall another
Thirteen week renewal

Day One

Marygrace's first day of preschool tomorrow
Don't let her drop her snack
Lose her pencil or be hurt by someone
Who doesn't want to be her friend

The Reverend's Daughter

The reverend's daughter was not
Allowed to listen to the Mamas and Papas
Record where they were fully clothed in a
Bathtub on the cover it was already an
Oldie by the time we were teenagers
She was kind of my first date when we went
To the musical in the city with a mutual friend
Though neither of us at least I did not think that
At the time still I remember her head on my
Shoulder as we rode the late night train home
Our clothes dripping wet from the
Downpour we ran through

In Recent Memory

For the first time in recent memory
More students on campus were reading
Books than talking on cell phones
It was a near perfect weather day
Which may bring out the best in people
Or perhaps the sun caused an atmospheric
Condition that blocked phone reception

After the Dishes

After the dishes are washed homework done
Laundry switched from washer to dryer
Dehumidifier emptied lunches made
Computer shut down alarm keyed in
Outside lights off nightlights on
Clothes arranged for the morning
Water bottle filled alarm clocks set
You still look as good as the first time
I lay beside you in the dark

The James Earl Jones Affair

I think my wife is having an affair with
James Earl Jones the eloquent actor whose
Speech at the end of *Field of Dreams* leaves
Me misty eyed the luxurious voice that gives
Life to Darth Vader the Great White Hope
Answers her cell phone every time I call and
Pretends he does not hear my
End of the conversation

A Chauvinist's Explanation as to Why the Sexes Should Not Commingle at the Mall

Women walking through a mall
Are thinking, "Maybe someone is having
A nice sale on shoes"
Men walking through a mall
Are thinking, "Look at all these women
I will never see naked"

Picasso's Model

She is unlike anyone who
Ever posed for Picasso with
Her eyes and ears and nose and
Breasts all in the correct places
Proportions and quantities sitting
Arms crossed pensive look after
The third and final sitting he shows
Her the portrait she is disappointed
When it looks just like her and
Captures the moment
They will never believe she
Sat for the great Picasso

Regeneration

If the cells of my skin have
Been constantly replaced
By new ones as the old ones
Die and fall away
Did you ever really touch
Me after all

Looking at the Photo of Kenneth Koch After His Death

In the cover photo his black hair
Is just starting to gray and the
Black rimmed glasses still perch
On his nose he wears a turtleneck
Shirt while deep in thought in the
Later pictures the hair is all gray
Glasses gone turtlenecks replaced
By ascots did you ever have trouble
Filling in the pages of your notebook
Or did the images form a deluge that
Left the pages sodden and your mind
Throbbing from the wringing of your brain

Dichotomy

Women walk around malls with
Younger versions of themselves
You can tell what the older one
Looked like in her youth
What the younger one will become
They feel both pride and envy
Each wanting the other to
Stay a little longer

I Lost a Poem Today

I lost a poem today
I thought I would remember it
So did not stop what I was doing
To write it down
Now it is gone
I have no idea what it was
What inspired it so it is lost
Among the many poems unwritten
For someone else to find cold and alone

Future Tense

Wherein the grown up Hermoine Granger
Leaves Harry Potter behind to become
The next bond girl in the third post Brosnan
007 epic shedding her wand and so much more
As Harry fights the demonic forces with
Symbolism of biblical proportions

Smuggling Tapes

Beatles master tapes stolen thirty years ago
Have been recovered by police in Amsterdam
Reel-to-reel tapes much harder to steal or
Smuggle than today's sessions which could be put
On a computer chip and purloined just about
Any way even swallowed to be recovered later
I wonder what effect that might have on the
Sound quality to have traveled the entire
Length of a human digestive system
Better to take chances with the
Brittle reel-to-reels

Juxtaposition

In the same issue of *The New York Times*
Polio makes a comeback in India
People turning away the vaccinations
As they travel from door to door
Fearing the rumors that the tiny droplets
That brought almost full eradication
Are actually part of a secret government
Population control initiative that will leave
The children sterile meanwhile in
Yellowstone National Park rangers fear that
The public will believe a television commercial
For an over the counter health product
Suggesting that the Old Faithful geyser uses
Metamucil to maintain regular eruptions

Without the Benefit of Cloning

Douglas Herrick needed neither
Cloning nor cross pollination
To breed the half rabbit half antelope
That became the legendary mythical
Jackalope as elusive the snipe and
Bigfoot the joke of a Wyoming taxidermist
Who saw a rabbit sitting near a pile of
Discarded antlers
Had a cat rather than the rabbit happened by
Herrick might have invented the more
Mainstream cantaloupe

What Benjamin Spock Left Out

You do your best
With your kids and
Hope they are
Successful enough to
Afford the therapy to
Undo the damage

Artful Blindness

The blind model is not
Embarrassed when she sits for the
Art class for hours in the nude
She does not see them seeing her
Or whether their sketches look like her
Or like someone she would rather be
The artists too are relaxed more than
They usually are when a model
Drops her robe before them

Tree's Place

The artist made blue the predominant
Color in the painting of the woman
Sitting at the table hunched slightly
Forward leaning out the window
The blue so rich and captivating
It takes a long time to realize that her
Bare right breast also blue is
Resting on the table

Endangered Species

For 19.95 you can adopt a dolphin
Wolf or Siberian Tiger you send the
Money and they send you certificates
And booklets and stickers but they
Don't actually send you the animal
Which is sort of good since they
Are endangered already and
Hard to care for in captivity

Old Roll of Film

If I found an old exposed undeveloped
Roll of film from my past
Would I recognize the people on the prints
Would the places look familiar
Memories flooding back like a
Volcanic eruption or would it be like
A box of old postcards at a flea market
Pretty pictures with vague impersonal messages

The Last Automat

I was young when I first saw her at the 42nd Street automat
It was a Horn & Hardart restaurant where you put coins in a slot, opened the little door,
    and took out the food
Which was then replaced by identical portions served by anonymous hands
She sat with a cup of coffee and a small pile of nickels which she unconsciously
    played with as she sipped
Her look was that of someone who had not been in the city for long but wanted to belong
She looked through me to the symmetrical rows of windows
Wondering perhaps if she should splurge and get the lemon meringue pie or maybe
    if she can take the disappointment of another audition
She became suddenly intense and wrote furiously on a folded napkin with a yellow pencil
The automat was deafeningly empty and I could hear her pencil scratching as she wrote

The few other patrons opening the little doors to remove chicken pot pie and egg custard
    had either missed their trains
Or had no particular place to hurry off to
Coffee spilling from the dolphin spouts lasted forever like the Tin Pan Alley dreams of
    those who sipped it from the thick cups

The girl with the coffee and the nickels and the pencil
Sees herself gliding across the great stage of Radio City
Or becoming a disembodied voice drifting from cathedral radios like Fanny Brice
    or Gracie Allen
Or as the ingénue in a black and white epic in movie houses with giant screens and
    majestic lobbies
I turned my gaze from her for a moment, distracted by a cross street bus
When I looked back her napkin and pencil and nickels were tucked away and she
    made her exit

I returned to the automat frequently always with a pocketful of nickels but she never
    appeared
Now the last automat has closed and almost nobody noticed

Charcoal Drawings in the Park

The first thing you notice is the way he uses the young girl's eyelashes as
the focal point for the sketch

She is not really known for her eyelashes but when he finishes the sketch
and the young girl holds it up, it is true, the eyelashes are the essence
of her beauty

When the little man started the sketch it was doubtful that it would resemble
her at all

Some of the features just did not look quite right

But just like the discordant notes of a fugue or the bitter in a sweet recipe
everything pulls together and seems to fit as one when he shades the dark
lines with his fingertips

And the young girl is pleased and contemplative as she admires his work

She is glad that he did not sketch her below the neckline

For she is shy about her looks, self-conscious, as are girls her age who never
quite expected all that nature wrought

She tilts her head to the left, her right, and smiles the gentle smile when she
examines the sketch

It is like looking into a mirror for the first time

She unfolds her crumpled bills and counts them out carefully, paying the artist
who rolls the sketch with a sheet of tissue paper

The girl is thinking of how she will never see the artist again, nor he her, yet
she will remember him always from the sketch

It saddens her to know that he has no reminder of her yet she knows that this is
how it must be

That he must stay here and she must forever move on

Even when the warm rains of summer wash the charcoal from the park and
his hands

Becoming one with the dust from her feet

Twisting Unicorns

Perhaps his dexterity in twisting balloons
Into a host of mythological and zoological creatures
Has its roots in the hours spent toiling in MIT's labs
None in the crowd could detect the advanced degrees in physics
Or the passion for the classics-the masters of the Renaissance-the
    thinkers of the Enlightenment-images that flash in and out of his
    brain
Or the time in the Hawaiian sun studying marine biology
His wife by his side, money a low priority in their lives
He creates his latex menagerie for the onlookers near F.A.O.
    Schwarz or when the sun is just right the Central Park zoo
He knows instinctively how far to inflate and how many twists to make
Dogs and ducks and rabbits come quickly, effortlessly
But the unicorn never comes out just the way he envisions it
It is always the horn, the angle never quite right
Still amid the yellow cabs and blaring horns and carnival afternoons
He twists unicorns, wrinkled dollars pressed to his white-gloved palms
He is a hybrid, part maitre d' part well dressed circus clown
With his black tuxedo, colorful sneakers, and big paper flower
They watch in silent awe munching street cuisine
The hands dutifully twisting
They do not notice the patchy flesh in the shade of his pork pie hat
He first detected the melanoma on a Wednesday surprised that his
    developed so quickly
He remained on his city streets his twisting becoming legendary,
    more precise
The unicorn remaining ever so elusive
His name in the *New York Times* obituary went unrecognized
But they knew the face like their own reflections in a mirror
The living eyes and dimpled cheeks of the forty-six year old virtuoso
And knew too that there should be balloons of all shapes, sizes, and colors
Flying over Fifth Avenue released like a million branch bearing doves
    spiraling toward the sun but there was
Only, shrinking ever so slightly on a snow covered subway grating,
A solitary unicorn, horn erect in angular perfection
Unnoticed in the chilly New York haze
As the street vendors stood unerringly still in perpetual motion

A Broadway Poem

Overture

The first Broadway show I ever attended was for my thirteenth birthday something
I wanted more than anything else
I had listened to the original recording of *Jesus Christ Superstar*, a two record set in a
    brown and gold sleeve over and over
Until it sounded scratchy from the cheap tone arm needle
Though we ate at Mama Leone's we walked by Jack Dempsey's restaurant
Where the old fighter emerged from a limo and shuffled inside as we hurried to the
Hellinger Theater for "King Herod's Song" and the Crucifixion

Act 1

The year I turned fifteen I saw five Broadway shows taking the train to the city
Claiming ownership of the streets and record shops from Fifth Avenue to Times Square
We would get half price tickets for four or five dollars at Duffy Square and I would
Read *Variety* while waiting on line

Intermission

When I was in college my mother and I would
Go to Broadway shows for our birthdays
Hers in December mine in June
We went to mostly musicals and had dinner at the
China Peace restaurant on 44th or 45th Street

Act 2

Now tickets cost one hundred dollars and I have taken my wife only twice
My *Variety* subscription has lapsed
The shows I fell in love with have been in revival and film adaptations
I listen to *Superstar* on CD and go to summer stock where there are no marquees and
The ghost lights are forever dark

Waiting for Ralph

As I stand on Madison Avenue waiting
For the express bus that will take me to the end of the line
I cannot help but wonder
How he held on driving
Into everlasting rerun retirement
Ralph Kramden the everyman
Destined to always be a step behind
And never smart enough to stay away from the next
Crazy hair-brained scheme

Handy housewife helper-
Uranium mine in Asbury Park-
Glow in the dark wall paper-
No-cal pizza-
Parking lot for the drive-in theater-
And the $99,000 Answer hamina-hamina-hamina

Best friend Ed Norton
Engineer par excellance in subterranean sanitation knew
     he was not
Destined to get ahead but
Was not smart enough to stay away either so he waits for Ralph
Married to Trixie, former Burlesque star, who was never
Afforded the same importance as say Ethel Mertz or Gloria Stivic
Or Blanche Morton or even Betty Rubble in TV foursomedom
Yet she too waits
Waits for Ralph

Long suffering Alice tired of looking at
That icebox that stove and those four walls
Pines for escape even the one way trip to the moon
That never quite materialized
Through it all though she knew that she was the greatest
And that some day there would be a happy ending for
Everyone at 328 Chauncey Street, Brooklyn USA
So she waits for Ralph

The sprockets worn out of the classic thirty-nine
They all moved to Miami Beach
A new Alice and a new Trixie
Old Alice not wanting to relocate

Ralph wanting the new Trixie all along
There was color Ralph and musical Ralph and
In the seventies mustachioed reunion Ralph
Then lost kinescope Ralph
Weight ballooning and shrinking
Norton as fidgety and rubbery as ever
Old Alice returned old Trixie did not

Tired of waiting for Ralph
Norton won an Oscar traveling with a cat
Alice periodically reappeared as a sitcom husband's
Acerbic mother-in-law-of-mine
Trixie, shut out from the reunions, settled into a happy life
On the uptown side of the bridge from Bensonhurst

As the sun sets with a bang and a zoom
I wait for Ralph
Knowing that when the full moon
Rises beyond the New York skyline
There will now and forever be
Ralph-oh-Ralph-Ralphie boy!
And the night will again be ours

Composite Sketch

It was the summer Johnny Carson hurt his back on an exercise machine
    and Shecky Greene filled in a lot
They never let Ed McMahon fill in when Johnny was off although they
    used to let Doc sit in Ed's chair
We would stay up late to watch them or Dick Cavett or Jack Parr who was
    back or comedy shows with Norm Crosby and his malapropisms
The NBC station would sign off the air after Johnny Carson although
    Tom Snyder was around by then
On the weekends there was a late movie show usually in black and white
    on another local station
A skinny girl in pink shorts sat on the stoop hugging her drawn up knees
We did not speak much or walk up the hill or around back to the laundry
We did not get to know each other at all and have one of those summer
    things that would last forever even after miles separated us
Had we, we might have exchanged school photos each year, the little ones
    you clip from large sheets of identical images
It was the year of the great flood
Susquehanna mud still caked the second story eaves and lattice work
Four by eight sheets of gypsum board were hauled in to replace the washed away
    plaster in homes
Gutted of possessions-clothes, books, records, letters from lost loves-shoveled
    and bagged and piled neatly at the curb
You said, "Give money to the Red Cross this year instead of sending Christmas
    cards"
It was the summer of Watergate-Sam Ervin, John Dean, John Mitchell, Judge Sirica,
    the one armed senator, and all the rest
Of clandestine nights and day-long hearings as a nation lost the innocence regained
Years later the hero security guard had fallen on hard times
It was the summer of the first Olympics with tiny gymnasts flipping, flying,
    and tumbling
And the swimmer with medallion after medallion of gold
It was the summer of Nixon resigning and Ford being sworn in as we drove along
    the interstate in a Buick
You said, "You are a witness to history"
The skinny girl still sitting quietly, long fine hair or was it close cropped
Still in pink shorts it seems to me and a white top
We never sat in the darkness, fingers barely touching, wondering what is American
    Pie anyway
Then chasing the white truck always deliberating then laughing nightly as we
    selected the same two flavors and shared them and saved the sticks
It was the summer of climbing a mountain in the Buick to a beach in the clouds

Of finding flat stones to scrape the location and date upon and slide under the
  back seat
Of creeping down ever so slowly hoping the brakes would hold as others passed
  on the yellow line
It was the summer of pulling in the distant clear channel broadcast on a
  small transistor by night
Of looking for the syndicated top forty countdown by day
Of tracking the chart positions of "Alone Again", "Brandy", "Leroy Brown",
  "My Love", Paul Anka's comeback, "Beach Baby"
And all the rest that meant so much then and mean so much now
Of finding bargain treasures in discount stores
Of weeks on your couch in those years but not later
Of porches and stoops and faces and voices known so well and now long gone
  and the endless promos for the new fall season and *Laugh-In's* last laugh
And now you are gone as well
The skinny girl is grown and I have no photo
Just this poem which will some day yellow and crumble then vanish
Just as Nixon died his melancholy death
Just as terrorists spilled Olympic blood
Just as test patterns became part of the stratospheric landscape
And just as the air you last breathed eternally recycles and we all exist
  for just a while longer

You Were Not Born

The leaves had turned early the year you arrived
It was not the first time the leaves turned early
The change in the leaves surprised neither of us
While the change in you surprised only you
The leaves, most feel, are more beautiful when they mature
The true beauty has always been there of course, one year's leaves
    predicting the next year's buds as they float to earth
You were not born when I bought Matchbox cars for 55 cents and
    comic books for 12 cents and Batman cards for a nickel
Those were the days when G.I. Joe protected the free world and
    kids' faces were not on milk cartons
You were not born when JFK and MLK and RFK were felled by
    assassins' bullets
You were not born when I watched Neil Armstrong step on the moon
You were not born when Nixon resigned and Carter smiled and Reagan
    won by a landslide
You were not born when the troops returned from Vietnam bringing peace
    with honor or for the psychedelic posters that said, "War is not healthy
    for children or other living things"
You were not born when "Crocodile Rock" and "Time in a Bottle" and "Cat's
    in the Cradle" topped the charts
Or for the concerts at the old Wollman skating rink in Central Park
You were not born for the Miracle Mets or when I watched Hank Aaron hit
    his 715th homerun or when Chambliss went deep for the pennant or when
    Bucky Dent homered into the Green Monster at Fenway Park or for Reggie's
    three homeruns on consecutive swings against the Dodgers
You were not born when the Beatles broke up or when John Lennon was shot
You were not born, yet all of these events occurred around me and I was alone
    and now you are here and
We cannot change history any more than we can stop the leaves from turning
Still as we sip our 50 cent cups of coffee I wonder what all of that history
    means since you were not there

October Song

At one point in time I called this "Different Worlds"
But that title seemed trite even though it is a recurring theme
We knew of course that we could not go home
But the feelings were so strong we had to return you and I
To the place beyond today
The first moments brought back so much of what we had left behind
Some by choice, some through a divine intervention eluding our grasp
    but not our souls
Still doing those things we used to do in places remembered
Something was different
The warmth, the safety, the anticipation were calling for an end
New people and places and feelings
We each may have had fleeting moments when we thought we
    were soulmates
And we likely really were ever so briefly
As our paths continually crossed but never merged
The promise quickly faded
A newborn understanding matured
And we joined hands to walk together
One last time

Welfare Island

My maternal grandfather, Morris called Morrie, had one leg
The other was amputated at the knee
I always assumed it was related to the series of strokes that confined him to Goldwater
    Memorial Hospital
Home to most of my clear memories of him
The hospital had green panels on its exterior and sat on Roosevelt Island
Also known as Welfare Island
There was no tram connecting it to Manhattan in the days when
My grandmother would take a combination of three subways and busses each way
To the man seven years her junior, partners in an arranged marriage
Sometimes he was in an old wooden wheelchair rather than his more familiar metal one
I never knew why
Heavy shadow on his face and black horn-rimmed eyeglasses
One time a van brought him to our house in the country
I must have been about seven and asked my father why so many of the
Tools in our garage were covered with newspaper
He explained that many of them belonged to my grandfather
And that it would make him feel bad to see them here rather than in his apartment
I knew that meant he would never leave the hospital for good
A decade after my grandfather's death when a modern housing complex opened on
    Roosevelt Island
I took the space age tramway across the East River, alongside the 59th Street Bridge
And walked around eventually arriving at Goldwater Memorial Hospital
Not realizing at first that I was on the island of my childhood visits
But soon bombarded with melancholy memories of
My grandfather's horn-rimmed glasses, five o'clock shadow, wooden wheelchair, and
    missing leg

The Photo of Kim Phuc

On June 8, 1972 when nine year old Kim Phuc was running through her burned out
   Vietnamese village
With napalm eating away her flesh
I was three years older than she and would soon be living with a friend while my family
   was between homes
We spent our days at the Putnam Plaza shopping center
Idly browsing in the Book and Record, Hallmark, Ben Franklin, Barkers, and eating
   thirty-five cent slices of pizza on sheets of waxed paper
We would listen for our favorite songs on WABC while making whirlpools in his
   back yard pool and
Stay up late watching old movies and *Johnny Carson*
Had I been born even six years earlier I might have been
Sent to Vietnam to listen for popular songs on Armed Forces Radio with Adrian
   Cronauer
How would my life have been different were I sent amid the rice paddies and agent
   orange
Rather that spending weekends with the Boy Scouts
Heating cans of Dinty Moore beef stew over campfires
And acting macho with little pocketknives and imitation military canteens
Worrying about raccoons getting into our packs as we slept in
Pouring rain in tents without floors
Along Candlewood Lake thinking we were the first to ever stage a successful snipe hunt
I would not have handled being in country very well
My feet would have ached as I can never find comfortable shoes
I could never have reassembled a striped rifle being inept even with Legos
None of the older boys in our neighborhood went to Vietnam as far as I knew
I might have handled it as a reporter for *Stars and Stripes*
But what words would I have found to describe Kim Phuc
Whose photo became a symbol for a generation and whose scars became triumph over
   the unspeakable
While I moved into a new house and to the next grade
Still not knowing where Southeast Asia was

Dateline Dallas

The earliest memory I can attach a date to
November 22, 1963
I was with my grandmother walking along the Grand Concourse in the Bronx
My grandfather must have been at work
Perhaps at the Flagg Brothers store on the street with the clock in the sidewalk
We might have gone for a few groceries or to Woolworth's down the hill towards the
    elevated subway
She said the streets were unusually empty
I had no concept of anything being out of the ordinary
We strolled a block west at one point, eventually returning to her apartment on the
    Concourse
After a while the big black rotary phone that sat beneath the cuckoo clock rang
She turned on the television
I sat on the floor, she on the couch crying softly
Grandma fell asleep at one point
I stayed on the floor not knowing the magnitude of a president being assassinated
Watching all the same
We talked of that day many times during the decades that followed
A bond between a grandmother and a grandchild
Many years later, four years after my grandmother's death
I obtained a tape of the live broadcast coverage of that day in 1963
As I listened to it alone I was overcome with emotion
I sat in my dimly lit basement and felt the pain that my grandmother must have felt that
    day
It was as if the voices on the tape, including a young Dan Rather, were telling the facts
    for the first time
I became choked up and knew that I was experiencing what my own grandmother had
    back in 1963 as she
Looked over my head at a black and white television screen filled with
Images of her world forever changed

A Day's Hard Night

When the Beatles first appeared on *The Ed Sullivan Show* I was happy to just stay up late
enough to catch a glimpse of Topo Gigio the mouse puppet
I bought the picture sleeve 45 RPM of "Let it Be" in 1970 when I was ten but
It was a decade later in a run down dormitory room on the 12th floor of Columbia's John
    Jay Hall that I became captivated by the quartet
Every night at 11:00 radio station WTFM played a half hour of their music
Phil and I and occasionally Mike would have instant coffee and listen as Dean Anthony
    played track after track
Phil would have his feet on the little square refrigerator
Waiting for songs on which John Lennon sang lead while
I preferred the catchier Top 40 hooks of Paul McCartney
On an old turntable in his room Phil had a Lennon record with a label on which
John turns into Yoko is a series of photos
On December 8 I was on the phone with Marie, Dino in the background playing WTFM's
    rotation of contemporary pop tunes
He broke in with the news that John had been shot and later that he had died
As events unfolded we would learn that Howard Cosell had made the announcement on
    Monday Night Football
Cosell who himself tried to recreate Beatlemania with the Bay City Rollers on his ill
    fated variety hour
It was late and Phil was awakened in his room next door by the commotion in the hall
"F—ing world," was all he could say before retreating behind his closed door
The next morning a sign in a window in the building across from ours read, "I heard the
    news today, oh boy"
A few days later while a vigil was held in Central Park in what would become Strawberry
    Fields
Phil and I sat in an obscure campus library
Pausing briefly in our separate study carrels each knowing the other had done the same
Then continued working into the night

Creature Features

Saturday nights my brother and I would watch *Creature Features* at
8:30 on channel five
We would turn off the lights and watch
The glow of the set burning our eyes in the darkness
Channel eleven had *Chiller Theater* with animated opening graphics
Where a six-fingered hand arose and pulled the
Letters into its bloody pool

Creature Features always had the better movies
The black and white ones with Boris Karloff and Lon Chaney and Bela Lugosi
Made by Universal in the 1930's
With the classic characters like Dracula, Frankenstein, and the Wolfman
Frankenstein of course was actually the old scientist not the monster

There is a scene where the monster is walking along and
Crushes the doll of a little girl
I first saw it when I was seven and it
Haunted me like a half dream half memory even more than
The old blind man in the cabin who tries to befriend the creature
It felt as if my own cherished trinket had been lost

Horror movies did not have to be in color before the public
Developed an insatiable taste for red blood
Even the oldest version of Nosferatu
Sent chills in living breathing black and white
Now the horror movies are more graphic and less scary and
Nobody even bothers to turn the lights off

Eradication

During fifth grade when we returned our signed permission slips to relieve the
    school of liability
They lined us up in the auditorium
To roll up our sleeves and be injected one after another
With the new vaccine that would prevent us from getting German measles,
    Rubella, as it was called on the TV commercial with the umbrella
The doctor used something that looked like a gun pressing the barrel
Against one pale hairless arm after another and pulling the trigger
Like a marksman knocking tin cans from a distant rock
Today with the fear of AIDS nobody would use the gun no matter how sterile
And would instead use the traditional syringes like we got jabbed with
Years earlier for regular measles, the ones without the umbrella
There was no fear of AIDS back then but we would all experience the
Bloated cheeks from mumps and the itchy oozing chicken pox
That would be smeared daily with Calamine Lotion
Each right of passage oddly welcomed for with each came a week of
Daytime television *Jeopardy* with Art Fleming, *Let's Make a Deal*, *The Newlywed*
    and *Dating Games* and sitcom reruns and cartoons
Now the games have been replaced by talk shows with sideshow freaks and
Wealthy hosts and twenty-four hour news and home shopping
And nobody gets measles or mumps anymore or even chicken pox very often
While I wonder do you control your body or does it control you?

Orientation

I was not enrolled in the first college class I entered
It was like one of those scenes that happens in a movie but not in real life
I had finally completed getting signatures in all of the little slots on my course approval
    card
A gust of wind tore it from my hand hurling it into larger and larger loops
Each time I bent to pick it up
Repeating the motion until finally depositing it in a grating outside the window
Of an occupied classroom
Necessitating my intrusion into the Ivy League class to go to the
Window and retrieve the card

There followed shortly the Statue of Liberty but not the top
A Yankee double header but not the bottom
Mixers with people I would never see again
Exchanging little more than our hometowns and prospective majors

On the first day of classes we were to assemble at the indoor pool
To pass a swimming test required by the rich alumnus who donated it
And who wanted to be able to sleep well should anyone ever drown
A few knew to bring bathing suits though for the most part it was
Line after line of flopping genitalia and pale buttocks jumping into
One end and emerging from the other

I had three incompatible suitemates one of whom
Ignored me any time we passed on campus
It was some time before I learned it was actually his
Twin brother to whom I had not been introduced

One afternoon after taking the subway south to the streets I loved
I purchased an oversized dictionary too big to be practical
Carried it back to school in a shopping bag
And displayed it on my shelf for four years

Everything was random in those days and in the
Years that followed
It was not until much later that I realized everything
Was interconnected
That philosophy was astronomy was
History was psychology and they were all part
Of something bigger
Like the twins who were one
And the oversized dictionary which contained no more useful words that the
Cheap paperback version and how
Climbing through the window was like jumping naked into the pool

Frank Messer Died

I heard on the radio that old Yankee baseball announcer Frank Messer died
I had wondered about him and where he was all these years since being unceremoniously
    dropped from the booth where he teamed with
Phil Rizzuto and Bill White to foster my lifelong passion for the game which I will
    always prefer on the radio
I knew he had done some college football and for many years introduced Mickey Mantle
    and Joe DiMaggio at Old Timers Day festivities
There is a music to those voices and to Bob Murphy's too
When the broadcasts start in spring training
Throughout college when the Yankees changed managers a lot but still managed to win
We would take the subway, the D train or the elevated line, to the stadium and buy
    grandstand seats for $2.75
After day games I would go to the luncheonette on Broadway across from campus and
    wait for
Night Owl editions of the newspapers to read about the game from which I just returned
There was a pleasure in reading about the game that was odd having been there in person
Even having kept score
There is a pleasure too in scheduling oddities like the time they had the Saturday *Game of*
    the Week on at 11:30 PM watching into the wee hours
Or the year the season opened in Japan, baseball on the radio during the 6AM drive to
    work
Back when Frank Messer called the games I would always remain until the last out
That seems less important now as does reading about a game I have just seen
Yet I will read about Frank Messer in the morning paper already knowing that he is gone

Bathypolypus Arcticus Octopus

In a darkened room on the lower level of the Cape Cod Museum of Natural History
Rests a small female Bathypolypus arcticus octopus which they call Polly
Captured by chance in a fisherman's net
She is white and about the size of a human hand with fingers outstretched
They keep it dark, lit by ultraviolet light and cold to approximate the
600 feet of ocean depth where the gestation usually occurs
She is perched on her eighty eggs and attached to a rock
They do not know exactly how old the eggs are
Just that after four hundred days have elapsed she will die and those that survive will
    perpetuate the species
My three-year-old daughter Marygrace looks to the sea creature with slight trepidation
"Why will she die? I don't want her to die," she pleads in her tiny voice
The museum worker, a serious woman with a turtle in her hand
Explains how rare it is for the octopus to be in captivity and how careful they are being
Not allowing any flash photography
She also offered that starfish are now referred to as sea stars and presented one to
Marygrace and her brother Justin for inspection
The little girl returned again to her desire that the octopus not die
Marie and I explained that it would not be for a long time (about a year the woman with
    the turtle predicted)
A child's concept of time made this a comfort
Yet she repeated, "Why does she have to die? I don't want her to die"
With a hint of the same fear her brother had the night before when he watched the
Crucifixion on the PBS remake of *Jesus Christ Superstar* and cried

Racing With the Moon

"Go faster, Daddy," Marygrace said, "I want to get home before the moon."
The moon seemed to be spinning with the clouds and she wanted
To race it home on a night during a summer of nights

The night of July 4th when we sat in the car
Watching fireworks over the lake
Children and teenagers walked by looking not unlike
I did so many summers ago when the
Moon was always full and the nights endless

It was the night of watching the children catch
Green sparkling fireflies and put them in a jar
Glowing like green moonlight

It was the summer of baseball games
    Little league
    Minor league
    Major league
It made no difference as the outfielders glided under the moonlight
Effortlessly as the white balls glimmered in the dusk

We did not win our race with the moon that night
It waiting over our house when we pulled into the driveway
Just as September arrived replacing our summer nights with the
Cool fall sunsets and chilly morning dew

Generations

My cousins Jenelle and Alyson and I have the same great grandparents
None of us knew our great grandparents though I came the closest
Being a little more than my cousins' combined ages
I know just one side of their gene pool so cannot be sure where Jenelle's
Wide eyes and Alyson's knowing smile come from

Our grandfathers were brothers thirteen years apart amid five sisters
Mine the older of the two and now gone
Theirs, the carpenter, still active and looking quite like his late brother did
From them we became in large part who we are

There is a desk crafted out of plywood by their grandfather
Passed from his children to my brother and me and to my children now
To sit at and do the homework that all generations avoid
We send our generations to seek more knowledge that those that came before

Alyson did not know the unhappiness of one school until transferring to another
Justin my son had the same experience at the same time though their ages are
About a decade apart much like Alyson's mother's and mine
Our children sharing personality traits

With all the knowledge of generations
I have a feeling that all of this means something
That I may never figure out

Hallmark Moments

When my son gets a greeting card he reads it out loud
He has a genetic predisposition to do this from the great grandmother
He never knew
My maternal grandmother's Bronx apartment building on Townsend Avenue was
    demolished
Years before my son's birth
He never saw the living room with the warped floorboard I would always trip on
The kitchen where she boiled chicken until the skin fell off and simmered matzo ball
    soup and borscht and made pot roast with carrots and potatoes
He never saw the couch that opened to a bed when you pulled out the bottom or the
    cedar chest
With the table top oscillating fan and the tarnished silver cups that nested inside one
    another
All moved to the suburbs where she would show my brother and me how to saw boards
    in the woods behind the house
My son's arrival was still a couple of years away when I last saw my grandmother in the
Nursing home, comatose, face red, breathing her last heavy breaths
Wishing to just once more hear her read the cliché ridden Hallmark verse of which she
    always believed every word

Living

The devastating waters of Hurricane Agnes had subsided the summer I started going to
　　Wilkes-Barre
But they had left a permanent record across the landscape of the region
I had a portable Panasonic cassette recorder that I would always have nearby
Recording sitcoms and radio station jingles and my grandmother either yelling in feigned
　　anger for my amusement or reading
Poetry from the collection of clippings she had amassed over the years
Our long drives to nowhere appealed to me far more than summer camps with log
　　cabins and murky lakes ever could

"That's the hospital where I did my training in the 1920's," she would say or
"I took your father to that airport for a plane ride once but I was afraid to go up and sent
　　him with a stranger" and one of my favorites
"When I was learning to drive I ended up crashing onto that dance floor in that building"

Grandpa meanwhile would take the car for gas and ask for "ten" laughing when the
　　attendant would ask, "Dollars or gallons?"
"This car won't hold ten dollars worth of gas"
As he approached his later years the attendant at his favorite station affectionately called
　　him "pop" and we would go a little farther and pick up
Kentucky Fried Chicken and take it home laughing even more when passing the garage
　　baring the owner's name "Heine Balz"

The neighborhood children would surround my grandfather as he sat on the front stoop
He would just sit in his chair and smile and watch them play
Inside he would sit at the oval kitchen table the one from the Bronx and play
Solitaire with the same deck of cards until the numbers wore off
He was the dish washer and coffee maker, how he enjoyed a cup of coffee
She would send him out for cigarettes and he would reluctantly say, "You get only one
pack"
Eventually she quit, tired of the constant haggling
What adventures we had rescuing Uncle Pete from the nursing home, finding previously
　　unknown roads that led back home, watching black and white movies until the test
　　patterns and white noise replaced the flickering images

Days went routinely by, but a good routine one of comfort and purpose
Believing that this life could rival any and secretly thinking that nobody else had it quite
　　so good

Living and Dying

"I can still see him taking his last breath," my grandmother said
On his death bed barely able to speak my grandfather asked for a cup of coffee
Which he would not have been able to drink
But that she later wished she had given him all the same

"I was hoping we would make it to our 60th anniversary"
He knew before anyone the end was approaching and had a
Final visit with his oldest friend Sam the president emeritus of the local bank
He cleaned out a lifetime of cancelled checks from the neatly stacked shoeboxes
In the bedroom closet

"I don't know what I am going to do," my grandmother continued, "but I guess people
    manage"
For the next seven years she was alone
I would take her on drives to visit relatives both living and dead
We would go to cemeteries to the graves where ancestors I never met rested
And to my grandfather's where she would one day rest as well
She would talk at the graveside telling him we were there
Then we would spread the bag of topsoil purchased at a nursery on the way
Around the base, she always wanting it to look just right

When we would get back into the car and drive away looking for someplace to have
    lunch she would say,
"Every day at one o'clock he would make me stop whatever I was doing to go for a
ride. Some days it would get me mad but how I would love to have one of those
drives now."

Living Again

Except once when I went with a rented van to take some furniture
(What a life comes down to bags for Goodwill neatly stacked for strangers
   to take what relations and friends do not want)
I had not been to Wilkes-Barre in the five years since my grandmother's funeral
As the years go by I want more and more for her and my grandfather to not be dead
So much of my life passed on with them so much of what I assumed always would be
So much too that I never knew

Thornton Wilder was right with his sparse staging of *Our Town*
"Do any human beings ever realize life while they live it?"
The hollyhocks and the bacon frying and coffee on a cold morning all the adornment the
   world needs

Now I travel the roads with my son
Though the traffic patterns have changed
Especially by the mall we used to go to and
We walk through the neighborhood
Strangers live in their apartment and in Grace and Joe's house and "up the junction"
   in Yolanda and Bill's too
My son looks forward to summer trips here as I did before him
We go to lunch and drop in on cousins
We visit my grandparents' graves and talk to them as
My grandmother had spoken at the graveside before me

Son of the Ciccus

I remember when I read "The Circus"
I was living in John Jay Hall on the Columbia campus we were
Well we had our own rooms but Phil and I were almost always together
The dorm had not been renovated yet and you needed to bend the
Prongs on electric plugs to keep them from
Slipping out of the outlets
With green water stains in the sinks and steamy communal showers
It was reminiscent of a downtown YMCA
Still we liked our rooms and the odd assortment of residents surrounding us
It was there I first read "The Circus" and wrote bad poetry and realized
Ever so slowly that poetry was not form but substance
That the things to include were the very things I passed by
Looking for things to write poems about

My poetry would have been better then and would be better now had I not
Failed at journal writing so many times
Nobody told me that the ordinary things would some day be extraordinary
I urge you to recreate your life from fragments and the scattered collection of
Places and dates it will all reappear
Nothing ever goes away it is the memory that gives it value
So everything and everyone lives forever
Is that from the Buddha or is it something else?

I know that cars run better if driven every day
That you should write in ink and save the lines you are tempted to discard
For they will in turn save you
I know that a third of a day is too much to spend sleeping unless you dream
I wonder if we will all live in a black hole some day or if that is where we came from
It seems the odds of our existence are stacked heavily for the house
So many ancestors having to meet to eventually lead to the one merger of
Sperm and egg to become the individual
I suspect that our estimate of a reasonable lifespan changes as we age
I suggest reading the philosophers and poets and books in hardcover
Eat spicy foods often but avoid foods with funny names

I suspect that I will get more from the 21st century than from the 20th
I lived through about forty percent of the 20th century and hope to see half of the 21st
That will depend upon numerous factors some beyond my control
Some of which I can pretend to influence
In the 20th century I read"The Circus" not understanding large segments of it
Or of me

Part II:

Summer Rising, River Flowing

Rising

My sister and I got to stay up later than usual
To see the late news after *The Dean Martin Show*
The anchorman with the Marty Feldman eyes on channel 28
Said that the Susquehanna River which ran between
My house in Wilkes-Barre and my friend Mandy's house in
Kingston was rising as we sat in the path of Hurricane Agnes

Mandy and I had seen yellowed newspaper clippings from the 1936 flood
In a scrapbook that her grandparents had kept but the
Thought of it happening again in 1972 seemed as
Far removed from reality as it could be as we finished the eighth grade and
Looked forward to high school in the fall

As I lay in bed I wondered if Mandy heard the river was rising or
Did she spend the evening listening to her 45s in her bedroom
We would meet in the morning I knew like we did
Every day at the Kingston side of the Market Street Bridge
No matter how early I walked across she would already be there
We would go to the park and debate regular versus white pizza or
Red versus white birch beer and throw stones and acorns in the river

Where we had kissed just once and
Wondered when it would happen again
As the river flowed and summer would last forever

Luzerne Country Courthouse

From the window of our rent controlled apartment
We could see the features of the courthouse
Not the ground level but the upper half that looked like a
Washington DC postcard it was clear from the news reports
The sandbags piled to protect the building and the past it housed
Were now piles of mud and cloth drifting away like the
Records of our births near the turn of the century and our
Marriage over forty years ago

That had been stored in dusty file cabinets in the
Bowels of the building for our unborn great-grandchildren
To uncover when we too are one with the earth
Pages of antique ledgers wrinkled and blotted with thick
Fountain pen ink awaiting the short-haired clerk
Who will spread what remains on the cold hard floor
When the water recedes attempting to
Reassemble the past one page at a time

EBS

Until that day the Emergency Broadcasting System was just
A high-pitched noise that interrupted my favorite radio stations
To tell us "where to tune if it were a real emergency"
WILK was now the only station my transistor could get
They were talking more and more about how serious this was
Still the thought of our river even as its level approached 20 feet
Overflowing its banks like rice over the sides of a pot
Every time someone on TV cooked too much of it
Did not seem possible and I missed the sound of my
Favorite songs humming under my pillow

The sun was not quite up yet when I heard my father
Rummaging around the house
I watched him through the crack in my doorway as he
Stuffed all the pillowcases from the linen closet into
Each other I knew what he was doing from the requests
On the radio that men come with bags to fill with sand
To help reinforce the dikes he saw me watching and
Told me to go back to bed there was nothing to worry about

It was another of those times when
Adults wanted to believe we knew less than we did
Like assuming we did not know why we could not go to
A Clockwork Orange which was at the Paramount in the
Square or *Carnal Knowledge* when it was in town

Curfew

The river was rising over an inch an hour and I did not
Want to be on opposite sides of the Market Street Bridge
I wanted to still be out with the volunteers like when we
Piled the sandbags with the hope of finding her and
I felt for the first time like I understood how the men felt
When they pulled on their old army uniforms on
Memorial Day and Veterans Day and marched in
Parades for everyone to see even though they barely fit
There was something about a brotherhood of men
In dangerous situations

My dad had gone back out but told me to stay and be
The man of the house that there was a curfew and the
National Guard had everything under control
When my mom and sister were asleep I did what I had
Done before and slipped out the window of my room and
Into the night

The streets were empty and it was easy to get to the bridge
It was barricaded with sawhorses and streamers of that
Yellow tape police used to outline dead bodies or to
Keep people off of wet paint
Bill the cop was pacing back and forth in the headlights of
His squad car one of his looks and nods was all I needed
To turn around and head back home

The Lines Are Down

It was not so bad until the sun went down I could
Pretend all day that we had electricity and that
Everything was normal I would rest my transistor
To save the batteries but it was my only connection
To the rest of the world and I felt somehow that wherever
She was Mandy was listening too and that made me
Feel that we were together like when we listened to our
Radios in the park waiting for our favorite songs
"Lean on Me" "How Do You Do?" "Heart of Gold"

I must have picked up the phone a hundred times
That day sometimes dialing her number even though the
Lines were dead in the back of my mind hoping it would
Magically connect but knowing that even if it did
She would not be there to answer for no matter how hard I
Tried to ignore the reports I knew her side of the bridge
Had been evacuated and that her basement

Where we had lain on the floor doing homework and
Watching Mike Douglas when he had a good co-host
Was underwater and that she was somewhere else
Among strangers wet and lonely and
Hoping her batteries would not die

On the Air

I remember reading about a New York disc jockey
Murray the K who moved into a subway station to
Broadcast as part of a radio promotional stunt
I never did anything like that in the small Pennsylvania
Markets I passed through from one end of the dial to
The other hosting nothing more newsworthy than a
Supermarket grand opening or feeding reports from a
Local politician's headquarters on the first Tuesday
After the first Monday in November

Dial hopping to WILK was no better or worse than any
Of the other stops along the way and the last time
Something really important happened while I was
On the air well nothing really important ever happened
While I was on the air

Our downtown studios were much less than listeners
Imagined which is always the case
As the band of weather moved toward the state the
Light bulb over the control board blinked a
Steady cadence and the row of buttons on the phone
Showed all lines filled with incoming calls
People called radio stations for everything
"When is the shortest day of the year?"
"Who won the best actor Oscar in 1970?"
"Which state mines the most silver?"
I had never expected to flick the little switches
To activate the Emergency Broadcasting System
Tone in anything other than a test
The river was approaching 40 feet and had not yet
Crested with a third of the city underwater

We kept at it repeating what news we had in a
Short continuous rotation as our competitors
One by one were washed off the air their
Studios or transmitters flooded and dangerous
It was a matter of time until we too would be
Evacuated from North Franklin Street
None of us went home but to safer ground and
Unsophisticated telephone hookups to continue our
Mission for days if the miles of wires stayed dry

Officer Bill and the National Guard

Having grown up on the same streets I had been walking
In uniform for all these years made it more than a beat I
Knew every inch of the roads that sat below the water like
Atlantis as I rode in the boat with the National Guardsmen
Pointing left or right instinctively sensing where residents
Might be stranded in upstairs apartments

A few times we were jarred by eight-foot lengths of
Two by fours floating by from the Pittston Lumber Company
Helicopters hovered overhead carrying dignitaries and
News crews you do not turn down the National Guard
But I knew it would be hard everyone in town was a friend

Many surprised and stripped clean as the river crested at
Over 40 feet it was easier in Kingston where the faces were
Not as familiar but still the same as we continued through the
Water in the distance the surface of the Market Street Bridge
Still rose above the river level to the left a
Geyser squirted toward the sky as natural gas lines
Broke through the feet of sitting water

The Clothes on My Back

Yesterday morning I got dressed three times before
I found an outfit I liked enough to wear to meet
Jeremy at the bridge I would push dozens of hangers
Filled with shirts and pants from one side of my closet
To the other then slide the doors shut and start again
Rows of shoes under the bed
Drawers stuffed with socks and underwear
Thrown out at the first sign of age

I was in my nightgown last night when the
Searchlight bounced off our front door like
The top of a lighthouse the man in the uniform
Told us the river had reached 20 feet and would
Crest much higher we needed to relocate to the
Shelter at the high school if we had no place else
To go I pulled on my jeans with the little hole
In the right knee and a Moody Blues concert shirt

They were not among the clothes I had considered
Yesterday morning but the first I found when getting
Dressed to evacuate I treasure them now
They are all I have

Disinterred

At first it sounded like more warnings about the
Dysentery that would cramp our insides unless we
Boiled water or mixed it with Clorox but it
Turned out the word was disinterred for the caskets
That floated to the surface as the layers of ground
Blanketing them like comforters tucked in at the edges
Washed away leaving the decaying remains
Exposed as the boxes old and bent gave way

It was like a gruesome anatomy lesson
At the site of an archeological dig
Pieces spread out randomly to be meticulously
Reassembled at a later date
Trees and headstones lay flat on the ground
Nothing seemed vertical in the world
Raking human remains into piles away from the
Debris deposited by the river teeth falling from
Skulls hollow eye sockets staring back

Is there anything I can do but
Sprinkle them with holy water and wait to
Rebury them in pine boxes in unmarked graves or
Divide the bones equally among the
Empty coffins and give each a headstone
Hoping that when the green grass once again
Grows the earth will settle firmly back in place
And the horizontal and vertical will again coexist

North Street Bridge

Just beyond the Market Street Bridge the
North Street Bridge in ruins washed out
Sections one with instead of over the
Susquehanna one survives the other falls
It looked like one of those cartoons where
Wile E. Coyote chases Road Runner to a
Cliff and just cannot put his brakes on in
Time to stop the plunge to temporary oblivion

The courthouse in the distance looked the same
But somehow further if not farther
The river a field of poppies between the
Yellow Brick Road and the Emerald City
Crews looked from makeshift paths and little boats
Not knowing how or what to recover first
There were no bodies no starting point
On which to focus just the
Knowledge that something must happen

Tinker Toys

The little girl a few cots away from me clung to her
Cardboard cylinder filled with Tinker Toys she was
Several years younger than I and wore the pajamas
She was in when her street was evacuated at least I
Was able to get dressed as we left
Her hair looked like it needed a good washing I had not
Seen myself in a mirror for over twenty-four hours
And knew I looked twice as disheveled
Even though it was summer it felt cold at least
I did and my nose was running

My feet were uncomfortable in my sneakers
Without socks which were hanging on the end of
My cot to dry the workers promised a
Salvation Army delivery of fresh clothes soon
I wondered where Jeremy was everyone said
His side of the river was mostly safe

When we would line up for food I imagined it
September already and the line was for tasteless
School lunches that would be eaten just a few
Periods before home and lying on my soft bed
Doing homework and listening to the radio
For now we were just a replica of a
Depression era soup line barefoot and cold

Leaving Anatevka

In the exodus the refugees of all ages
Walked through the streets staring straight ahead
Most of the time as the river rose past 35 feet
Bags of hastily packed belongings
Most light not believing they would be gone long

Days later the faces looked the same after the
Water receded to 25 feet and falling
They returned to gather what they could
The boy pulled the red Radio Flyer wagon by the
Black handle his load consisting of less than
Expected a life reduced to a few identifiable trinkets
Covered by a plastic tarp

Blank faces passing in the midday sun
Pain exhaustion sadness did any exist without the others
The feeling of being violated though not touched
Not robbed by human hands learning that
Material things can be an extension of the body
Raped and left for dead

College Avenue

College Avenue is what we called it not River Street
Though that was its real name
With the stately old homes and thick trees it seemed the
Name it should have
The college seemed like an old ghost town even
Before the flood waters arrived
With just a few of us milling around during the
Summer term four guys in a three-month rental
With an old Rambler station wagon that we
Drove to higher ground when the evacuation signal
Pierced the air seven times in succession

Whether it was being young and still self-absorbed
Or just not paying much heed to the magnitude of
What had transpired on the streets where we had
Walked with virgins in the moonlight and ate
White pizza and drank bitter ale that tasted like
Urine smelled whatever the reason
When we returned after the waters receded
And did not find things the way we left them
It was like getting undressed before a
Mirror and finding an unfamiliar body under the
Layers of protective clothes

The overpriced textbooks on the bookstore shelves
Turned back to the pulp from which they came
Floorboards in the gym were no longer smooth and
Shiny but protruded in compound fractures
That only full amputation would cure

Carrol's Restaurant

We joked about how we now worked in the first
Drive-in restaurant you could drive up to in a boat
Inside the potted plants in their octagonal buckets
Dripped mud on the slippery tile floor where we
Waded through an inch of stagnant water that
Smelled like the restrooms the manager would make
Us clean when it was slow near closing time

I was assigned rags and a spray bottle of cleaner to
Revive the plastic seat cushions in the booths while
Cassie the counter girl who worked double shifts to
Support her adolescent daughter had a mop and one of
Those buckets with the ringer attached
We would lean against the mop handles while we
Smoked during our mandated fifteen minute breaks

The stuff we were cleaning was not much different
From what the regular customers left behind there was
Just more of it for Cassie it would be harder getting to
Work from the trailer park and would take longer
But then the world had expanded exponentially and it
Would take us all a while to catch up

HUD

Until this summer *HUD* was the name of a Paul Newman
Movie now the letters are ones I will never forget
HUD-The Federal Department of Housing and Development
Along with the number "one billion" the number of dollars in
Damage left behind by Hurricane Agnes
Instead of our home with the plaster walls and
High ceilings and antique tiles in the bathroom that
Mom bleached to perfection we live in
This anonymous trailer the seventh one in row eighteen
Our area is set up in rows others circle out like the
Spokes of a wagon wheel

I always knew our house from even before I could walk
By the lantern-like street lamp at the end of the
Driveway near our mailbox now I cannot even find my
Way home and if I enter the wrong door it really will not
Matter much anyway

All the things that made my home mine are gone
My clothes and stuffed animals the knickknacks in the
Living room the papers magnetized to the refrigerator the
Cluttered medicine cabinet shelves my *Tapestry* and
Superstar albums I try to remember that I am just one of
Eighty thousand without a home with still more than
So many others

Typhoid Mary Lives in the Square

The gutting and gathering had not slowed down
Even after days of dragging the piles of clothes and
Notions from Pomeroy's, S.S. Kresge, Woolworth's and
The other stores in Wilkes-Barre square
Contaminated boxes bottles tubes of medicines other items
Attached to their cardboard cards piled in front of the
Drug store a giant open air pharmacy

I was younger than most of the volunteers but
Nobody ever asked my age even when the
Red Cross or was it the National Guard lined us up
In a makeshift emergency ward
The nurse in the white uniform on my right and the
Bi-spectacled aid on my left were the only
Signs of cleanliness I had seen in days
Each pointed a slender syringe at me as if they were
Ready to let them fly towards the bull's-eye of a
Dartboard in the back of a corner bar
One dart was for tetanus not updated since the time I
Stepped on a rusty nail the other for
Typhoid which I thought existed only in old stories like
"Masque of the Red Death" and not typhus which is
Apparently from a different bacteria entirely

There was a perverse pleasure in feeling the
Fluid flow from the slim needles as they pierced
My arms simultaneously not unlike dragging the
Sandbags and pulling the debris from the storefronts
As if being in a foxhole with planes flying overhead and
Giving your friend your last cigarette

Checkers Returns

The driver stopped along Wyoming Avenue so I could
Walk among the displaced all I could see was Checkers
That little cocker spaniel the girls so loved when they were
Little and we picked him up at the Union Station in Baltimore
Dog's been gone for years and I had not thought of
Him for almost as long still those floppy ears and the
Wet nose he would rub on my good suits
Were all I could see in every direction as people
Talked and extended their hands I responded
Mechanically seeing Checkers staring back from
All of their pupils pull it together Dick

Tell them we will get them homes we will
Get them all home all of them
Home before the election before Christmas
The tattered clothing the destruction choppers
Flying overhead clear your mind Dick

Let them say what they will the political
Cartoonists who stretch my nose and give me the
Jowls of a Thanksgiving turkey to hell with
Them all and the democrats
The record is preserved like no president before me
Snap out of it Dick

I can still feel that dog tugging on my shoelaces
Checkers, come here boy

Nothing Rhymed

There was music playing in the background not the
Catchy Top 40 hooks from Neil Diamond and the
Carpenters but quiet music that our radio stations
Never played soothing and distant at the same time

The water had receded leaving the river itself
Normal but our park littered with random bits of
Cloth, wood, metal, ceramic, and unidentifiable
Materials along with dead carp caked with mud and
A pair of sneakers that did not match

I walked towards Mandy's street her house still
One of many in the distance
Rugs hanging in the sun to dry never to be used
Like the clothes and linens that would forever
Carry the indelible tattoo of the river from
Wash to wash

Against the tree with the peeling bark
Leaning haphazardly upside down
Paintings of the Virgin Mary and
Jesus Christ pulled from the rubble and
Put in the sun to dry

As I walked farther from the bridge
I could see her silhouette, long hair flowing
Jeans outlining her body as she pushed a
Too big for her broom through the silt and
Sludge and left her footprints in the mud
I knew as I watched her that our views of
The world just like our views of the river
Would never again be the same

Orfanella

Part III:

K-tel Presents Believe in Poetry

Brandy (You're a Fine Girl)

Eighteen months have passed since I
Last set foot in that harbor town but I can
Still see that chain of silver
Braided in the Spanish style
Encircling her neck shining and looking
Awkwardly out of place as she wiped the
Tables with her dirty bar rag and
Laughed at their dirty jokes and felt dirty
Jumping as each request for a new
Round was released in the
Stagnant salty air there was that

One night when the doors were
Locked and she thought she was walking
Home alone along the silent streets
I let my shadow stretch out
Just before her so as not to startle her
She stopped and turned around cautiously
We had the night that would
Turn into day and the day that would
Become goodbye just as I told her it would

As she went to talk I put my finger to her parted lips
I left more than that braided chain
In the town with one bar and the
One girl who could challenge but
Never defeat the sea

Alone Again (Naturally)

I have sketched that abandoned
Tower six or seven times in different shades of gray
Since I moved to this cheap attic apartment
Two years ago it is the only thing that
Breaks the monotony of the view
The clouds and the trees change around it
While it stays the same streams of
Orange rust forming irregular stripes
On the stones that were chiseled years ago
By calloused hands and carefully lifted into place

This is the first time I have
Seen any movement in the tower
The shadow of a man through the
Openings in the top not moving
Staring out to sea though no
Water is nearby
Standing there for hours listing
On occasion but generally steadfast

Finally when even the day's
Shadows are feigning to fade with
The sun he begins his descent
Disappearing from my view
Reappearing after a long while at street level
Becoming one with the horizon

It Never Rains in Southern California

Eastbound Greyhounds can bring you
To a better place than westbound 747s
Especially when they are heading for
Places you have already been
Where the only stars are in the sky

She would have kept her word I was
Sure of that nobody would know
How she found me that one time
She came looking asking me to
Come home they would believe I
Was weighing offers making far
Different choices that those before me

The road into town was the same as
I remembered it with a few more
Trees perhaps and the sun illuminating
Yards and storefronts more than before
It was foolish to have expected her to wait
For me to find a new life in the old a lifetime away

The lies become the truth and the
Truth becomes the past
And the Free Electric Band becomes
An American band on the run
Looking for a sound in the silence

Saturday In the Park

The little man selling the ice cream
Has been here since the park was
Young they have no idea that he
Makes the ice cream himself from a
Recipe he learned in the old country
When he was young and not as small
Nobody thinks about what he does
The rest of the week nor would they
Notice he was missing if they came to
The park on any day but Saturday

He is as much a part of their day
As the secret paths they walk on or
The kisses they exchange on the rock in the
Shadow of the building on the east side of
The park where the man with the
Ice cream always appears in the same
Spot with the same four flavors
Chocolate vanilla strawberry and pistachio which
Is his best but his slowest seller in this
Country he is the only vendor who
Sings the hot dog man does not even
Speak very much and the pretzel man
Always seems busy adjusting his
Propane or fixing his umbrella

When they buy their cones each week
They do not think about who the ice cream
Man is or even realize that
They have seen him for twenty
Saturdays in a row and often hum
His songs in their heads during the week not
Knowing what the Italian lyrics mean or
Why they hear them

Bad, Bad Leroy Brown

For all its reputation I knew the
Southside of Chicago could be no
Worse that what I had seen in the
Midnight Cowboy world of Times Square
And 42nd Street where the cars were as shiny as
The knife blades that cut flesh like scaling a fish
When Alabama Slim came for revenge

Each night Doris perched at the end of the bar
Under the hair she bleached but did not need to
Skirt too short for a barstool
Makeup heavier than needed but still
Shy of looking like someone trying to
Look younger than her years
The big man who appeared and
Straddled the stool next to her
Looked like a delivery truck with
Legs where wheels should have been

He made her move leaning towards her like
A mudslide on a rainy night
She crossed her legs and took a long drag on
Her cigarette before crushing it out
Leaving just the butt with bright
Red lipstick on it

It is hard to chronicle what happened next
Arms legs bottles and chairs became a congealed
Mass flying in all directions diverting attention
From the real damage
When Leroy was carried out by the people who
Would no longer call him friend
He was leaking blood from more places than
Jim Walker when they rolled him off the pool
Table and out the door so they could rack 'em up
For another game

I wiped down the bar and
Swept the glass locked what remained of the
Door and decided to look for better days
In the Alabama rain

Photograph

No matter how many times I
Rearranged the photos in my
Big album with the magnetic pages
Hers was always in the front
There were newspaper articles and
A few ribbons won for participation
In unskilled events or academic
Competitions meaningless certificates for
Trivial accomplishments but her photo
Always came first even though
I knew I would never see her again
When youth fades faster than brittle
Newspaper clippings it is easier to ignore the
Hands on the clock the ever-tuning calendar pages
To retreat to the familiar past which has taken on the
Hue of nostalgia the soothing comfort of an
Old friend's letters the voices that never fade
The photograph that keeps her frozen in time

Yesterday Once More

Songs from the radio played in
My head all the time even when the
Radio was not on they were the
Songs that played in the background and
That blared from the dashboard and
That appeared in big headphones and
Tiny earplugs the songs came in all styles

One after another Charlie Rich and the
Beautiful girl who left and Tom T. Hall
Loving ducks and trucks and pictures of
His friends Marvin Gaye got it on while
Gladys Knight got on board Edgar rode
For free and Angie a-Angie said goodbye

Through it all the teen idols in and out of
Our lives passing through Gatsby's fruit
Processor in on Friday out dried and
Shriveled by Monday a few hints of
Pulp to be carted away one pubescent pop
Prince following the other faces ripped from
Tiger Beat and taped to the wall
Young girls and boys alike believing the
Heartbeat was truly a lovebeat dreaming of
Having a hit record or marrying Tony
Defranco who charted three times after
Donny Osmond's voice changed

Daisy A Day

It was called penny candy but
Cost less when they first started
Coming here for sheets of buttons and
Root beer barrels he always held the
Door for her even when they were
Young and just learning to flirt
With each other when he went to war
She continued to come in and sit at the
Counter sipping chocolate sodas through
A straw reading *Life* and *The Saturday
Evening Post* existing in her own
Norman Rockwell world when he
Returned he went to work at the factory
Like all of the men in town
Always coming to the store then going
For their walk to the hill with the
Wildflowers when he started coming in
Alone it was hard to look at him
Without feeling the emptiness seeing him
Walk among the wildflowers that
Continued to grow

Jazzman

You need to be old to be a jazzman
Black poor and blind to be a jazzman
Wait that's a bluesman he bends forward
Slightly at the waist and shoulders when he
Plays sounding too precise too exact with
Every note when the lights go down around
Him and the acrid cigarette smoke encircles his head

Once poised the music is the only thing that seems
To be in motion the jazzman seems to have been
Carved from fine stone placed on the stage as
If on a museum pedestal
As he plays the muffled chatter and clinking
Glasses slow to silence the sweet seductive
Music meeting the silence with one of its own
Five seconds seem an eternity
Broken by a crescendo of reckless abandon
A climactic rush of uncontrolled passion

Gyspys, Tramps & Thieves

Occasionally I wonder when I
Pass a group of transients or
Migrant workers if she is among them
If she looks at thirty like she did
At sixteen in Mobile when we took the
Bottle behind their wagon while
The old man shouted fire and damnation at
The sparse crowd who watched the dance
Swigged the snake oil and tonics that we were
Lubricating her inhibitions with I never felt
Guilt never felt anything at the time
They took the public for what they could
I guess I did the same
Each night's faces the same as the other
By Memphis I moved on she no longer the
Mysterious stranger with the dark eyes
Wide as a tambourine
The old man had said nothing
Those last two days he did not have to
I knew it was time I moved on

Paper Roses

Marie Osmond was just about
My age when she hit with
"Paper Roses" that I mistook for love as
The lyrics went Anita Bryant the
Orange juice hawking homophobe had the
Original hit but inspired no
Adolescent crushes like the
Innocent voiced Mormon with the
Toothy brothers from *The Andy Williams Show*

This was a few years after thinking that
The Partridge Family really sang and
Played when it was really just Mrs. Partridge
And Keith who did and who were really related
She was a famous movie star shocking her
Old fans playing a widowed mom in a sitcom
Driving around the country in a psychedelic
School bus singing "I Think I Love You"
That slick pop confection with the
Harpsichord that holds up over time like the
Family itself as opposed to *The Brady Bunch*

How any misguided puberty drenched boy
Could prefer Marcia Marcia Marcia over
Laurie Partridge the debate ending when those
Paper Roses seemed so real to me

Radar Love

The music on the radio seemed to be in sync with the
Sound of the car on the highway
We were heading east for no particular reason
I kept it no more than ten miles above the speed limit
It felt like more the music got louder on its own
Filling in the gaps in the conversation we were having but
Paying no attention to it felt like an important trip we
Were on both knowing that we were really just killing time

Stopping for plates of greasy cheeseburgers and fries
Then turning back west and driving slowly to ballads on the
Rock and roll radio and making plans that one of us
Always believed in more than the other
When we finally stopped driving late enough
Dark enough tired enough I would leave the ignition
Key in the one click position so that the radio would
Still play and we did not have to talk our tongues
Being otherwise occupied the heat from the engine
Dissipating in the dampness of night

Please Come to Boston

I could be happy here if she would give it a try
The wind off the water is cold when I walk
Alone along the harbor far from Tennessee
Inspiration comes easily here it might be
The history or the quaint nature of everything
New England the thought of her alone in

Knoxville where her art will
Never be seen and where my songs were
Listened to but never heard is enough to
Make me want to go back but not enough
To make me leave

I think if I get to L.A. I can make a life
She would share even though it would not be
The same ocean the water would surely have
Merged at some point in its travels through the
Lunar cycles

Carefree Highway

When at sixty Gordon Lightfoot was hospitalized
With a condition described as an abdominal weakness
I wondered what went through his mind
Did he have songs that he was too weak to write
And did he lose them in the darkness of night
Did music play in his room until he was finally
Released in the same month that Lucy Grealy
Autobiography of a Face author died

I had heard of neither of those events
Until more than a month after they took
Place finding out simultaneously had I not
Stumbled randomly through the universe finding
These facts he would still be hospitalized and she
Still living with a deeper understanding of life and
Beauty than most of us ever achieve
I do not control the fates and destinies
But it is our knowledge that gives events
Meaning when truly the tree that
Falls in the forest as we travel the carefree
Highway around the next bend at seventy
Miles per hour makes no noise if
We are not there to hear it

Beach Baby

The beach seemed much smaller
Than it used to be when we
Laid side by side on the sand and looked for
Clouds on the periphery of the
Blue sky over the dock with the
Peeling paint and the low diving board
Seaweed floated around
We were unaware of those around us
Were they unaware of us as well

Just two kids in a summer like
Any other except that we had
Each other in June and July hoping
August would never arrive for it
Would inevitably turn to September
And we would not longer be here
We would once again be anonymous
Faces with the fading tans
The girl next door and the boy who loved her as the
Leaves fall from the trees and the night falls early
In the town where the beaches close after Labor Day
The subdivisions reemerge and who we are means
More than who we were when the sun was orange
Long after our tans fade to winter's pale white flesh

Shambala

The green highway sign said Shambala was
Three miles away which brought with it
Images of *Lost Horizon* that old movie
So I turned the old silver VW bus off the
Interstate at the next exit where the
Population density was about the same as
Mayberry or one of those towns where
The houses all have porches and the
Nearest store with a national name is
Forty miles away eight track tapes

Of "I'm A Drifter" and "Long Lonesome
Highway" played over and over all of us
Solitary travelers seeking love and leaving it
Behind music played in my mind as I
Moved from town to town each uncharted
Road leading to another some nights sleeping
With only the silence of night for company
Others a distant stranger's hair touching
Mine as the twilight becomes night and a
Heartbeat and warm breath recede into
Daylight when I will move on the same song
The one that penetrated my dreams swirling
Around my brain as I think of
Returning but never do

Crocodile Rock

She was leaning against the jukebox
The first time I saw her it was one of those
Big bright Wurlitzer jukeboxes with
Row after row of great songs and
Where you could see the record being
Put in place after you put your money in and
Made your selection she was with two other
Girls always they were with two other girls
The other two had shorter skirts and were
Facing the machine pointing to the new songs
That were added each week when the
Jukebox man came and changed a few of the
Selections I wanted to talk to her but knew
I would not, not then she being with two of
Her friends and I with two of mine that was the
Problem at every soda shop in the country
Everyone was always with two friends

The three girls including mine in the longer
Skirt with the poodle on it walked towards
A table the two friends clearly the leaders
Mine was the quiet one who was with them
To complete the threesome which is what I
Found attractive about her that and the way
She held the sides of her glass as she sipped
Her cherry coke through a straw
I sat watching her for a long while
Knowing she would leave before
I would get up and approach her
I would talk to her the next time she came in
Or maybe the time after that

Seasons in the Sun

Popular songs in the twentieth century
Could make people cry movies and TV too
In the twenty-first century people do not cry
Dismissing the sentimental as
Outdated and old fashioned it was not always
This way I cried when the girl died at the end of
Sunshine and Brian Piccolo too and when
John Boy left *The Waltons* and when they
Buried Grandpa Walton

When Bobby Goldsboro sang "Honey" I had
Not experienced loss but cried
When the daddy died in "Keep on Singing"
And when "Patches" took over the farm
That choked up feeling would appear
When Peggy Lee asked "Is That All There
Is?" and the first two versions of "Last Kiss"

There were others old and new in the twentieth
Century as we pass through the "Side Show" we
Call life all hoping for the center ring feeling like
The twins with two heads but one heart with
No choice but to follow the tears that flowed
Freely when "Seasons in the Sun" made its
Meteoric rise up the charts as millions of
Others cried as well

Orfanella

Notes About the Poems

One of the things people who attend my readings and workshops tell me they enjoy is hearing the stories behind the poems. In somewhat abbreviated form, here are a few notes about the poems in this collection.

"The Gatherers" was inspired by a photograph I came across in a *Life* magazine collection about the sixties. I found the perspective of the figures in the photo thought provoking and inspiring.

"Action News" was written as an attack, or at least a comment, on the sensationalism that has changed the face of journalism

"When They Caught the Son of Sam" is a poem I first wrote many years ago, but was unhappy with. When I revisited it, it went through many drafts before reaching the form it appears in here. It is an attempt to capture that feeling of pure innocence and simplicity we have before the reality of life sets in.

"Tales from the Sour Cream Sierras" is a sequence of poems inspired by the legendary resorts of the Catskill Mountains. The great culture of the European Jews was preserved there and became part of America's culture as well.

"Primary Sources" is a poem about the poetic process. A participant in a poetry workshop told me one night that she could never figure out how to end her poems. One of the exercises we had been working with was writing a poem about poetry. This poem is the result of thinking about those ideas.

"Barry Manilow Doesn't Suck and Other Sound Bites" came to be as the result of a year-long exercise in writing short poems. I wanted to attempt to capture the little moments of daily life with the compressed language of poetry and the immediacy of a diary. The thirty-seven poems that make up this sequence were culled from over three hundred that I wrote in a "poem a day" journal. Sound bites are those short clips of tape that appear in radio news broadcasts which attempt to capture the essence of a story in about thirty seconds.

New York City has provided the inspiration for many of my poems including several in this collection. "The Last Automat" was written in response to yet another cultural icon vanishing from everyday life. "Charcoal Drawings in the Park" is the first poem I ever wrote that I thought was "good." It was when I first realized that I might just be able to use words to "take a photograph" of something. "Twisting Unicorns" was inspired by an obituary for someone I may or may not have ever seen. "A Broadway Poem" is a tribute to the way the shows we see on the Broadway stage tend to stay with us forever. "Waiting for Ralph" was written as an unabashed love letter to the greatest television comedy ever.

Starting in the summer of 1972, shortly after my grandparents retired to Wilkes-Barre, Pennsylvania after many years in New York, I began spending summers with them. More than two decades later, I began jotting down random memories of those summers and as I did they formed a mosaic of memories that became the poem "Composite Sketch" and led to my thinking of poems as composite sketches. I also became more deeply aware of how important those simple summers were to me. I am additionally "grateful" to this poem as it led me to eventually write the series of poems in *Summer Rising, River Flowing*.

As you grow older, perceptions change. Things that were integral to our lives we take for granted and others around us have never even heard of them. "You Were Not Born" is an attempt to bridge the gap, or at least acknowledge its existence.

"October Song" is a simple poem that I have often tried to dismiss as not one of my better ones, but somehow I found myself drawn back to it each time I did so. Maybe it is the simplicity that I find myself enjoying.

"Welfare Island" is a poem intended to preserve the few memories I have of my maternal grandfather. My three other grandparents lived well into my adulthood (and their eighties), and provided me with much inspiration as well as a hopeful optimism as far as genetics.

I have always liked the idea of seeing poems as photographs designed to capture a moment. "The Photo of Kim Phuc" was inspired by the famous photo from the Vietnam era that became a symbol for a generation. I wanted this poem to symbolize the limited vantage point I had during that time period.

"Dateline Dallas" and "A Day's Hard Night" were inspired by the two defining events of my generation, the assassinations of John F. Kennedy and John Lennon.

"Creature Features," "Eradication," "Orientation," and "Frank Messer Died" all consist of "growing up" memories.

My children are at the heart of both "Bathypolypus Arcticus Octopus" and "Racing With the Moon". "Bathypolypus" was for me, one of those magical times when words did exactly what I wanted them to do.

"Generations," "Hallmark Moments" and the trilogy that consists of "Living," "Living and Dying," and "Living Again" all stem from the sense of urgency I feel to preserve family history as well as the never ending amazement I find in seeing how one generation affects the next.

"Son of the Circus" is a poem I like to use at the end of my poetry readings. It is both an attempt to examine my own "philosophy" and a tribute to the late poet Kenneth Koch without whose inspiration none of this would have been possible.

The eighteen poem sequence "Summer Rising, River Flowing" was inspired by the images that have stayed in my mind since the summer of 1972 when I saw firsthand the destruction done when Hurricane Agnes swept through northeastern Pennsylvania. The Susquehanna River overflowed its banks leaving over one billion dollars in damage, thousands homeless, and entire towns underwater. I had trouble finding the right point of view for these poems until I decided take on as many different narrative voices as necessary. At that point, everything started to pull together and it was a very exciting experience.

"K-tel Presents Believe in Poetry" is another sequence of poems written around a theme. In early adolescence, popular music becomes the soundtrack of our lives. In the days before music videos told people what images they were meant to get from songs, we listened day and night for our favorites to come on the radio. These poems take their titles from some of the songs that were such an important part of my life that they sound as fresh to me today as when I first heard them.

Orfanella

About the Author

   Lou Orfanella believes that writing is a strip-mining process in which physical, emotional, and spiritual truths are unearthed as one digs deeper and deeper into one's storehouse of memories and experiences. He is a New York based teacher and writer who holds degrees from Columbia University and Fordham University. He teaches at Western Connecticut State University and in the Valhalla, New York school district. His work has appeared nationally and regionally in such publications as *Teacher Magazine*, *New York Teacher*, *English Journal*, *College Bound*, *Discoveries*, *The New York Daily News*, *World Hunger Year Magazine*, *WordWrights!*, *The Danbury News-Times*, and many others. He offers individual instruction and group workshops on topics including poetry, memoir, journalism, fiction, and family history. He can be contacted by email at LORFANELLA@hotmail.com.

Orfanella

108

Printed in the United States
19089LVS00004B/223-300